Canon EOS R5 User Handbook

The Complete EOS R5 Manual with Illustrations for Beginners

By

Walt Leaburn

Copyright © 2023 Walt Leaburn,

All rights reserved

Canon EOS R5 User Handbook

Table of Contents

Chapter 1: Getting the Lay of the Land 5
Getting Comfortable with Your Lens 5
    Attaching a lens 5
    Removing a lens 7
Setting the Focus Mode 8
Adjusting Diopter Correction 9
Working with Memory Cards 10
Exploring External Camera Controls 11
    Front View 11
    Back-panel controls 14
    Right side controls 16
Choosing Shooting Settings 20
Using the Quick Control Screen 21
Restoring Default Settings 23

Chapter 2: Taking Great Pictures, Automatically 25
Getting Good Point-and-Shoot Results 25
    Use proper lighting for professional photography 25
    Use filters and presets for professional photography 25
Flash Exposure Compensation and FE Lock 26
Exploring Your Automatic Exposure Options 28
    Scene intelligent auto mode 28

Chapter 3: Picture Quality and Size 31
Resolution (Image Size) 31
Understanding the Image Quality Options 32

Chapter 4: Reviewing Your Photos 36

Playback 36

Enabling Automatic Picture Rotation 38

Viewing Picture Data 38

    File Information mode 38

    Highlight display mode 39

Rating 39

Erase Images 41

Memo Audio Quality 43

Protect Images 44

Cull Images Conveniently 46

Chapter 5: Getting Creative with Exposure and Lighting 48

Introducing the Exposure Trio: Aperture, Shutter Speed, and ISO 48

Exploring the Advanced Exposure Modes 50

Setting ISO, Aperture, and Shutter Speed 53

    Adjusting aperture 53

    Adjusting shutter speed 54

    Controlling ISO 54

Choosing an Exposure Metering Mode 55

Applying Exposure Compensation 57

Tonal Range 58

Chapter 6: Downloading, Organizing, and Archiving Your Picture Files 62

Sending Pictures to the Computer 62

    Connecting the camera and computer 62

    Starting the transfer process 62

Downloading and Organizing Photos with the Canon Software. 63
   Downloading with Canon Transfer 63
   Browsing images with the Main Dial.............................. 64
Organizing pictures 66
   Moving Images.. 66
   Moving Images by Folder 67
Processing RAW Files 68
   RAW Processing (RAW/DPRAW)............................... 68
   DPRAW Processing... 71

Chapter 7: Capturing Video 74

Getting Started 74
   R5 Video Overview... 74
Movie Recording Quality 76
Movie Cropping.. 79
Movie Self-timer... 80
Remote Control 81
IS (Image Stabilizer Mode) 81
Zebra Setting 83
Overheat Control.. 85
Movie Autofocus Menus.. 85
   Movie Servo AF... 87
   Movie Servo AF Speed 87
   Movie Servo AF Tracking Sensitivity 88

Chapter 1: Getting the Lay of the Land

Getting Comfortable with Your Lens

Attaching a lens

My suggested lens mounting technique emphasizes safeguarding equipment from unintentional harm and reducing dust infiltration. First, if your camera doesn't have a lens attached, choose the one you wish to use and undo the rear lens cover. Next, store the lens you intend to mount vertically in a slot in your camera bag, which is safe from harm but still easily accessible. The lens's rear element is protected until that point by releasing the rear lens cap, allowing you to remove it off the back of the lens at the last second.

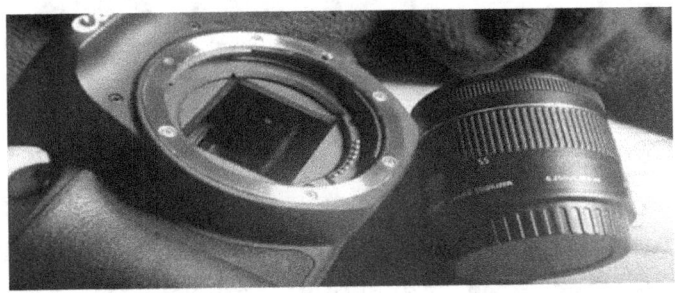

After that, turn the body cap toward the shutter release lever to remove it. When using a camera without a lens, you should always mount the body cap because it helps keep dust from getting into the camera, where it could collect and perhaps end up on the sensor. (While the sensor-cleaning system functions properly, the less dust, the better.) The body cap also guards against injury from intrusive things, such as your fingers if you're not careful, to the sensitive sensor.

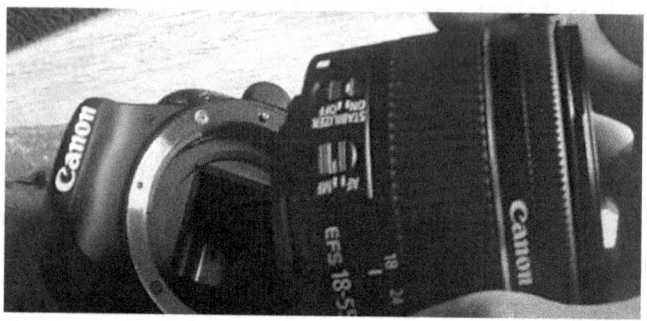

After removing the body cover, the lens should be mounted on the camera by aligning the raised red alignment indicator on the barrel with the red line on the camera's lens mount. Next, the lens should be turned away from the shutter release until it is firmly in place. Next, set the stabilizer switch to On and the AF (autofocus) focus mode switch. Finally, if the lens hood is bayoneted to the lens with the hood facing inward (which makes the lens/hood combo more portable), twist it off and remount it with the hood facing outward. A lens hood prevents accidental bumps, stray fingerprints, and flares from extraneous light entering the front element of the lens from outside the image area. It also reduces flare.

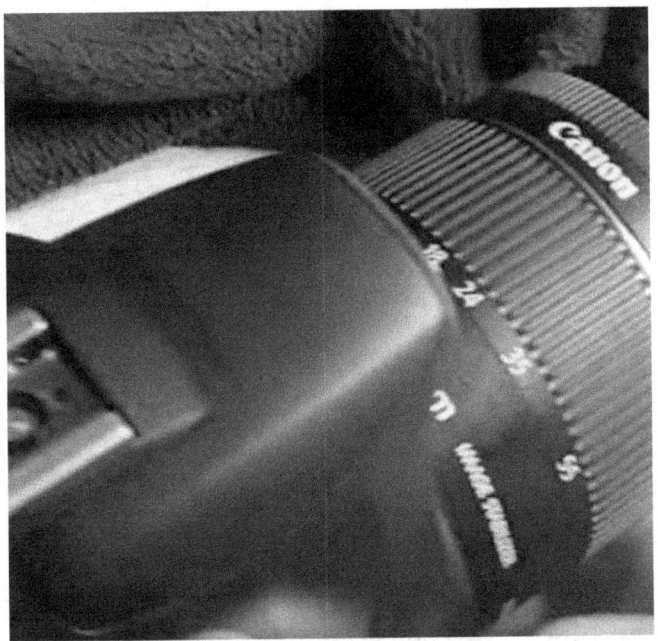

Removing a lens

Turn the lens in the direction indicated by the arrow while pressing the lens release button.

Detach the lens by turning it until it stops.

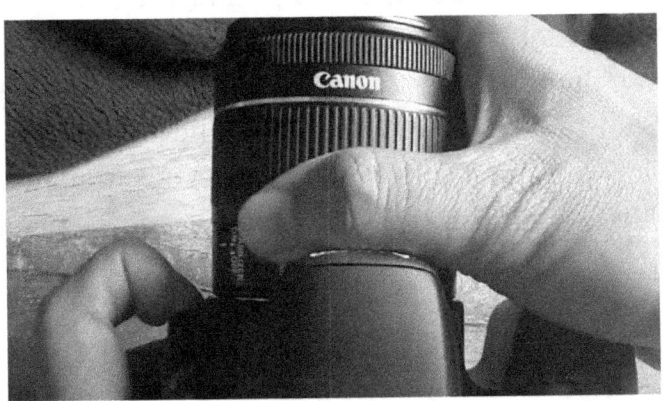

Put lens covers on the lens you just removed.

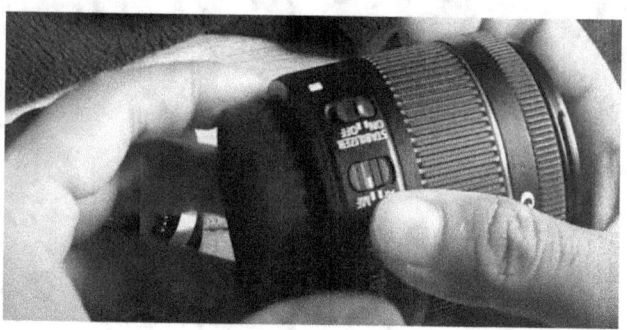

Setting the Focus Mode

By adjusting the AF/MF switch on the lens installed on your camera, you can quickly switch between automatic and manual focus. You must still select a suitable focus mode, which instructs the camera when to focus when AF is engaged if you're shooting in a semi-automatic mode.

Access the viewfinder or the two LCD screen versions of the Quick Control display as previously mentioned, then select the AF Operation (focus mode) icon to change the autofocus mode. In the visual Quick Control screen, it may be found directly to the left of the Metering Mode symbol and second from the top in the left column of the other two views. Next, choose either the OneShot or Servo AF option, as indicated by their labels. Both options won't be accessible if the lens is in manual focus; instead, an MF indicator will be displayed in place of the symbol.

The focus modes are:

- **One-Shot:** This setting, known as single autofocus, locks in a focus point when the shutter button is only partially depressed. If the image is sharply focused at the active focus points, green boxes will appear; otherwise, orange boxes will emerge. The focus will stay locked until you let go of the button or take the photo. When your topic is largely stationary, this mode works well.

- **The Servo AF:** When you partially depress the shutter button, this mode, also known as continuous autofocus, sets focus. However, it continuously scans the frame and adjusts focus if the camera or subject is moved. For taking pictures of sports and moving subjects, utilize this mode.

Adjusting Diopter Correction

A little optical refraction in the viewfinder is frequently helpful for those with less-than-ideal vision. You might not require any correction from your contacts or glasses, but if you wear glasses and prefer to work without them, you can benefit from the camera's built-in diopter adjustment, which ranges from -4 to +2 correction. Turn the diopter adjustment dial to the viewfinder's right while looking through the viewfinder with the camera turned on until the indicators are sharp.

Working with Memory Cards

Two of the three methods for making a blank memory card for your camera need to be corrected. Your choices, both right and wrong, are as follows:

- **Transfer (move) files to your computer:** The old picture files are erased from the memory card, leaving the card blank, when you transfer (rather than copy) all the image files from the memory card to your computer (either using a direct cable transfer or with a card reader). Theoretically, this method does not identify or lock out any areas of your memory card that have become corrupted or unusable since the last time you formatted the card. It also does not remove files you have designated as Protected (by selecting the Protect images option in the Playback menu). So whenever you want to create a blank card, I advise formatting the card rather than just copying the image files. Only when you wish to keep the protected/unerased photographs on the card for a little longer, much to share with friends, family, and coworkers, is there an exception.

- **(Don't) The format in your computer:** You can use Windows or Mac OS to reformat the memory card while it is inserted in your computer's card reader or slot. Don't! The operating system may not always organize the card structure in the manner preferred by the camera (in computer terms, an incorrect file system may be installed). Only by formatting the card within the camera will you know that it has been done correctly for your camera. This rule only deviates when your camera won't format a memory card that is severely contaminated. By first enabling the operating system to reformat the card and then attempting again in the camera, it is occasionally feasible to recover such a corrupted card. Set up the menu layout. Follow the steps below to format a memory card using the suggested method:

1. Input the MENU key.

2. Rotate the Main Dial to choose the wrench-shaped Set-up 1 menu.

3. Rotate the QCD-1 on the camera's back to highlight Format Card in the Set-up 1 menu, then press the SET button in the QCD-1's middle.

4. After deciding which card to format, press SET to confirm.

5. Rotate the QCD-1 to the OK position, then press SET once more to begin the format. If the card has been used a lot, it's a good idea to perform an extra thorough low-level "clean-up" format by pressing the Trash button first.

Exploring External Camera Controls

Front View

Your subjects will see the face of the camera as you continue to take pictures. There are only three buttons to press on the front of the camera, all easily reached with the fingers of your left hand, in addition to the shutter button and Main Dial, which are located on the top/front of the hand grip for the photographer. The lens itself has extra settings.

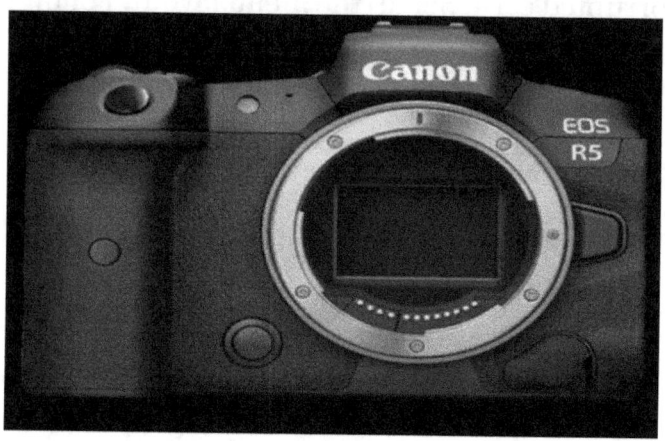

The other main components you need to know regarding include the following:

- **Shutter release button:** The shutter release button is angled above the hand grip. Exposure and focus can be locked by partly depressing this button (in One-Shot mode and Servo AF modes with non-moving subjects).

- **AF-assist beam, self-timer, and lamp controlled by a remote:** When necessary, this LED flashes to add more illumination and help with autofocus. This lamp also illuminates when the remote control is connected and when the self-timer is getting used to mark the remaining time until the picture is shot.

- **DC coupler cord hole:** To connect the DC power line to the camera through the battery compartment, this cover opens on the inside edge of the hand grip.

- **Hand grip:** This cozy handhold houses the camera's battery.

- **Remote control sensor:** Remote control sensor infrared signals from the Canon RC-6 Wireless Remote Control are used to start and stop video recording and trigger the shutter.

- **Depth-of-field preview button:** A preview of the depth of field is provided when the lens is stopped down to the aperture that will be used to take the picture.

- **Lens mount:** Each lens or accessory you mount on the camera will fit into this reliable flange using a corresponding bayonet on the back.

- **Lens release button:** Holding this button will unlock the lens, allowing you to turn it to remove it from the camera.

- **Lens lock pin:** When the release button is depressed to unlock the lens, this pin on the lens flange retracts.

- **RF lens mount index:** As you put your RF or mount adapter lens on the camera, align this mark with the complementary red detent on the lens's barrel.

- **Shutter:** While the camera is turned off, the shutter is closed, giving the delicate sensor some protection, especially when switching lenses. You should be careful to turn the camera off before changing the lenses because the shutter opens when it is switched on. When manually cleaning the sensor is the only time you want the shutter to be open without a lens connected.

- **Electronic contacts:** To enable electronic communication between the camera and lens, these contacts are connected to corresponding spots on the lens to enable electronic communication between the camera and lens.

- **Stereo microphone:** A single microphone is located on the front of the R5's camera, close to the AF-assist beam.

- **Remote control terminal:** You can add extras like the TC-80N3 timer remote controller or the RS-80N3 wired remote switch.

Back-panel controls

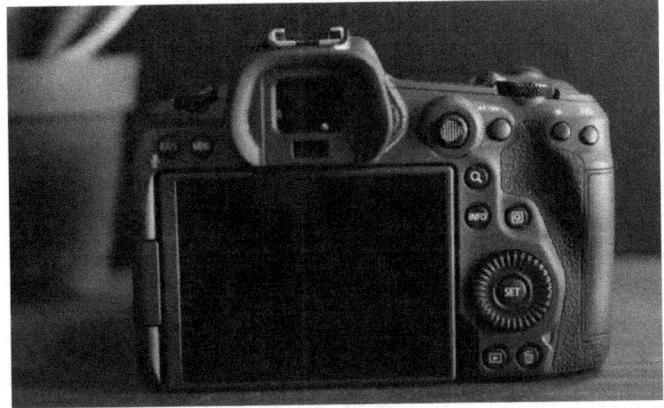

- **Menu button:** This brings up or closes the menu that is visible on the camera's LCD or electronic viewfinder. You can also use this button to leave a submenu and return to the main menu when using submenus.

- **RATE button:** This button has two different use.

- **Rating:** This button's default behavior with both cameras is to let you "grade" pictures while they're being played back. Pressing the button more than once while an image is being played back gives it a star rating of one to five or clears all ratings. In addition, you can assign the Protect function using the Playback 4 menu's RATE Button Function entry, or you can select the Erase Images behavior.

- **Voice message:** The R5's RATE button has a new microphone choice next to it. Instead of repeatedly pressing the button to apply a rating (or to Protect or Erase an image if you've redefined the button), you must hold down the RATE button for more than two seconds while viewing the image you want to add a voice memo. This second function is also available during Playback. Hold the button down as you record an audio memo for up to 30 seconds using the voice memo microphone on the camera's back, which is close to the LCD screen's lower-right corner.

- **Dioptric adjustment dial:** To adjust your vision, turn this dial while looking through the viewfinder.

- **Viewfinder eyepiece/eyecup:** You may frame your composition by looking through the viewfinder eyepiece. When you push your eye tightly up to the viewfinder, the soft rubber eyecup/frame surrounding it filters out extraneous light and guards against scratching your eyeglass lenses (if you use them). 5.76 million dots make up the electronic viewfinder on the R5.

- **Viewfinder sensor:** This sensor detects when an item, such as your eye or another object, is getting close to the viewfinder eyepiece. The camera automatically shifts between the two by default, but by using the ScreenViewfinder Display option in the Set-up 3 menu, you may set the camera only to switch manually.

Right side controls

- **Quick Control Dial 1 (QCD-1):** Used to navigate menus or choose shooting choices like f/stop or exposure compensation value. It also acts as a backup controller for various operations set with other controls, including selecting the AF point.

- **Quick Control Dial 2 (QCD-2):** The second QCD dial allows you to skip right from one major heading to the next when navigating through menus. For example, this will enable you to skip right from the Shooting menus to the AF menu and the Playback, Network, Set-up, and Custom Function menus without visiting each tab in each group. (To go from Shooting 1 to Shooting 2 to Shooting 3 and so forth, turn the Main Dial, which is located right behind the shutter button.) Other directional tasks are also performed with the QCD-2.

- **AF-ON button:** To activate the focusing mechanism without partially depressing the shutter release, push this button. This function enables you to lock exposure and focus independently when used with other buttons. For example, you can lock the exposure by halfway pushing the shutter release or pressing the AE Lock button; by halfway pressing the shutter release or pressing the AF-ON button, you can turn on autofocus.

- **AE/FE (auto exposure/flash exposure) button:** When you partially depress the shutter button while in shooting mode, the camera locks the exposure or external flash exposure. Press button one again to recalculate exposure while the shutter button is still half depressed. When you let go of the shutter button or capture the photo. Keep pressing the same button while taking pictures to maintain the exposure lock for later shots. While using an external flash, pushing the button triggers an additional preflash when the shutter button is only half depressed, enabling the camera to determine and lock the exposure before snapping the photo.

- **AF point selection button:** This button has two functions:

    - **AF area mode selection:** To switch between the various AF area modes, including Face+Tracking, Spot AF, 1-Point AF, Expand Area AF, Expand Area AF (Around), Zone AF, Large Zone (vertical), and Large Zone, click this button once, then hit the M-Fn button (explained shortly) again (horizontal).

    - **AF point movement:** In all AF area modes except Face+Tracking, this button will allow you to navigate the AF point or zone across the frame using directional controls like the Multi-controller.

- **Multi-controller joystick:** When shifting focus points, moving a zoomed area, browsing menus, and performing other actions, this joystick-like button can be moved in eight distinct ways. It can be pressed to turn a setting on or to confirm it.

- **Voice memo microphone:** This microphone is set up so you can record one or more voice memos, each lasting up to 30 seconds, while a picture is being played back.

- **Magnify/Reduce button:** This button has separate functions for Shooting and Playback modes.

  - **Shooting mode:** When using an AF method other than Face Detection+Tracking, press this button once to magnify the screen by 5X, 10X, and then once more to return to a 1X (full frame) view. You can move the zoomed region while the image is magnified by using the Multi-controller.

  - **Playback mode:** Press and then let go of this button. The QCD-2 will then be turned to the right to close in on a still image gradually. The Playback 4 menu's Magnification (apx) parameter allows you to choose the initial magnification out of 15 distinct increments ranging from 1X to 10X.

Zoom out to full-frame mode and then to views of 4, 9, 36, and 100 images by turning the QCD-2 to the left—Press SET to get a full-frame view of the presently selected image in either index or magnified view.

- **SET button:** This button acts as a control to activate or confirm your option when making choices.

- **Card slot cover:** To access the camera's two card slots, slide the cover toward the back of the device.

- **Quick Control (Q) button:** By pressing this button, the Quick Control screen, which is accessible when in Shooting mode, will appear. A new Quick Control panel appears when you're examining photographs in Playback, allowing you to protect or rate images, alter the jump method, resize, crop, rotate, and carry out other operations.

- **Access lamp:** This lamp indicates that the memory card is being accessed while lit or blinking.

- **Erase/Trash button:** In playback mode, pressing this button removes the image that is now being shown.

- **Playback button:** This shows the latest image.

- **The INFO button** alters the information shown in the shooting and playback modes. It's also utilized on some menu displays to open up more options or information.

Choosing Shooting Settings

If you fitted a lens, attached a new battery, and loaded a memory card before turning on the camera, you are ready to start shooting. A shooting mode, metering mode, and focus mode must all be chosen.

Press the MODE button on the EOS R5's QCD-2, which is situated in the center of the top-right corner of the camera. Then, press the left/right buttons to choose a mode or turn the Main Dial or Quick Control Dials. The current mode is displayed on the LCD panel on the top of the camera and the color LCD screen on the rear of the EOS R5.

Using the Quick Control Screen

Quickly changing any of the 10 distinct settings is through the Quick Control page. Use the directional controls to highlight one symbol and move to the next to access any modification; movement will wrap around between columns. Use the left/right directional controls or either dial to choose from the options shown at the bottom of the screen after you've highlighted the adjustment you want to make. You can tap their icons on the touch screen, as I mentioned. While evaluating your photographs, a second Quick Control panel is available.

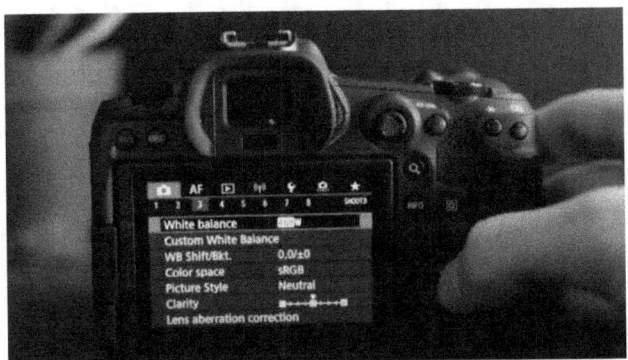

Your options in shooting mode are as follows:

- **AF Method:** Select the region of the frame that will be utilized for automatic focus.

- **AF operation:** Select between the OneShot and Servo modes.

- **Image quality:** Select from Large, Medium, or Small resolutions in RAW and JPEG file formats.

Choose Single Shooting, High-Speed Continuous +, High-Speed Continuous, Low-Speed Continuous, Self-timer: 10 sec., or Self-timer: 2 sec. from the drive mode options.

- **Metering mode:** Choose the region the camera will utilize to gather exposure data.

- **Anti-flicker:** This technique combats the flickering effects of particular lighting kinds.

- **White balance:** Choose from various white balance settings, including Daylight and Incandescent.

- **Picture Style:** As you shoot, apply photo-enhancing settings to your photographs.

- **Auto Lighting Optimizer:** Modify shadow detail in photographs with a lot of contrast.

- **Cropping/Aspect ratio:** Crop your photo to the 1.6X (APS-C) format, or adjust the aspect ratio to 1:1, 4:3, or 16:9.

Restoring Default Settings

It would be a good idea to ensure the camera is set to the factory defaults in the first place if you want to change from the default values. Even a brand-new camera might have altered its settings in the store or during a demonstration. But most of the time, you'll want to choose the Basic Settings and Other Settings options under the Set-up 5 menu's Reset Camera option.

Basic Settings restore the factory defaults for menu settings and camera shooting functions. Your camera will be set to One-Shot AF mode, Automatic Face+Tracking AF-point selection, Evaluative metering, Single Shot drive mode, JPEG Fine Large image quality, Automatic ISO, sRGB color mode, Automatic White Balance, Auto Lighting Optimizer Off, and Standard Picture Style regardless of how you've configured it. Any adjustments you've made to the white balance, flash exposure compensation, or exposure compensation will be undone, as will any bracketing you may have used. In addition, the Dust Delete Data and customized white balances will be removed.

The Other Settings option resets all other settings to their factory defaults, including those for the Root Certificate, Communications Settings, Shooting Information Display, Custom Shooting Modes, Copyright Information, Custom Functions (custom buttons and custom dials will be kept), Custom Controls (clears custom buttons and custom dials), and My Menu. Additionally, the Custom Functions 3 menu offers a

Clear Customized Settings option, while the Custom Functions 5 menu offers a Clear All Custom Functions option.

Following the Basic Settings menu resetting option, the following tables display the default settings. In addition, many (but not all) menu options (some menu items are functions rather than options) and camera options like Drive mode are included.

Chapter 2: Taking Great Pictures, Automatically

Getting Good Point-and-Shoot Results

Use proper lighting for professional photography.

Let's start with lighting for product photography. With good lighting, your product will look as it does to you in person, and your background will be unique. " According to Tony Northrup in an article for the digital photography school, a white background without light doesn't seem white in the picture; it appears grey.

Lighting for product photography comes in two flavors: artificial and natural lighting. Which configuration you choose will depend on the product you're promoting. For example, products with edible products, people, and apparel can be photographed using natural lighting, and these shots with a natural appearance can be used in social media settings.

Use filters and presets for professional photography.

You can tell the appropriate filter and preset are critical when you employ filters because your images appear too fantastic. Because the proper filter plays a crucial part in photographs, every photographer should possess the correct knowledge of filters. Filters are helpful, but if you use them excessively, you will appear very unprofessional. The moral of the story is to use filters sensibly. Filters reduce glare and reflections, the amount of light entering the lens, and more. Each lens filter has a distinct function that can improve how a picture turns out.

Flash Exposure Compensation and FE Lock

The FE Lock (the * button) can lock in a set flash exposure for a subject not in the center of the frame. Simply place the subject you want to expose accurately in the viewfinder's center, then hit the * button. Pre-flash ignites and determines the exposure. The FEL indicator, a lightning bolt with a * next to it in the lower-left corner of the display, is your reminder. The camera remembers the proper exposure until you take a picture. Press the * button once again to recalculate your flash exposure. Recompose your shot and fully depress the shutter button to take the picture when you're ready to shoot.

Without touching the flash, you can manually increase or decrease the exposure for the flash. In addition, you can access flash exposure compensation (FEC) in a few different ways when using any exposure mode other than Scene Intelligent Auto, which includes Program AE, Aperture-priority, Shutter-priority, Flexible-priority, or Manual.

- **Set flash exposure compensation (FEC):** Check your Speed lite manual to see if you can set the flash's FEC. Look at the sidebar that follows. You should be aware that once FEC is specified on the flash, it cannot be changed via the camera's controls.

If the Shooting Information screen is enabled, you can display it by pressing the INFO button until the screen appears. Then, hit the Q button, select the FEC icon on the Quick Control screen's far right side of the second row, and turn any dial to adjust.

- On the Quick Control screen, press SET. You might consider doing this if you prefer to make modifications using the touch screen or require the improved legibility that a larger screen offers.

- To access External Speedlite Control, locate it in the Shooting 2 menu, hit SET, and then choose Flash Function Settings if your flash is connected and turned on. Next, select the Flash Exposure Compensation icon in the screen's second row. If you were changing many settings from that screen, such as FEC, you might choose this option.

Flash exposure compensation and non-flash exposure compensation can be used in conjunction, allowing you to modify the quantity of ambient light captured while also adjusting the amount of light emitted by your flash unit. Remember to cancel the flash exposure compensation adjustment by going back through the steps you used to set it when you're done using it. Like with non-flash exposure compensation, the compensation you make is retained for the images that come after you make it, even after you've turned the camera off.

Exploring Your Automatic Exposure Options

Scene intelligent auto mode

Adding an exposure mode to an advanced camera that offers almost no user options may seem confusing initially because it effectively reduces a professional or enthusiast camera to a point-and-click camera. However, if you look closer, you'll see that there is a method to Canon's apparent insanity and that Scene Intelligent Auto is much more than just a trimmed-down version of Program mode. The term "Intelligent" in the mode's naming is crucial.

Only the camera controls the shutter speed and aperture while in P mode (explained in more detail below). Almost all other options are editable, including the metering mode, autofocus mode, and white balance. The camera will evaluate your scene in Scene Intelligent Auto mode, going so far as to determine whether or not your subject is stationary or moving, and then intelligently select the best settings without input from you. The camera may adjust the following settings:

- **ISO speed:** The camera will select the appropriate ISO sensitivity.

- **Picture Style:** The camera will select the proper settings when the A (automatic) Picture Style. It should be noted that Scene Intelligent Auto will not consider any adjustments you have made to the Auto Picture Style.

- **White balance:** This setting is predetermined and cannot be altered.

- **Auto Lighting Optimizer:** On in Scene Intelligent Auto mode at all times.

- **Color space:** sRGB is required.

- **Autofocus:** When you partly push the shutter release, the camera chooses One-Shot AF or Servo AF. The AF-assist beam is turned on whenever necessary, and the AF point selection is always automatic. You can toggle Eye Detection on or off by clicking the Q button, selecting the AF Method icon, and then pressing the INFO button.

- **Metering mode:** Always utilize evaluative metering.

The following options are available while using Scene Intelligent Auto:

- **Manual focus:** To choose the manual focus, turn the lens' AF/MF switch to Manual.

- **Touch focus:** If Continuous AF is disabled in the AF 2 menu, you can use the touch screen to tap on someone's face or another subject in the frame.

- **Drive mode:** You can switch between single shooting, high- and low-speed continuous shooting, Silent single shooting, Silent continuous shooting, and 10 and 2-second self-timer settings using the Quick Control screen.

- **Image quality and size:** Use the Q button to choose between RAW, JPEG, and other image sizes, such as Movie Recording Size.

The Scene Intelligent Auto mode's condensed four-tab menu layout includes two Autofocus menu tabs and some particular Shooting menu choices.

Chapter 3: Picture Quality and Size

Resolution (Image Size)

Less technical options are available for resolution:

- **8K-D (8192 x 4320):** The R5 is the only device that supports this wide-screen DCI format.

- **8K-U (7680 × 4320):** For the 8K video, this is the UHD format in 16:9.

- **4K (3840 x 2160):** Although there are now few options for content and displays, this ultrahigh-definition format is the future trend. Even if your goal is to distribute Full HD footage, you'll undoubtedly find yourself shooting 4K as you develop in the video industry. Many editors insist that 4K video converted to Full HD is superior to Full HD that has been natively captured. It is referred to as 4K-U (ultra-high definition).

- **4K-D (4096 2160):** The R5 is the sole device that supports this "wide-screen" Digital Cinema Initiatives (DCI) format.

- **1920 x 1080 (1080p):** This resolution, referred to as "full HD," is the highest shown while using the HDTV format. You can select this resolution to get the best image quality on most HD televisions and monitors. Use this resolution for your "professional" projects, particularly if you plan to edit and create attractive DVDs from them. However, as was already noted, the highest resolution uses the most storage space, between 235 and 685 megabytes each minute. A 16GB memory card can hold a collection of clips that total no more than 22 minutes of recording (using ALL-I compression with the R5) or 1 hour and 4 minutes (with IPB).

Understanding the Image Quality Options

The Shooting 1 menu's first choice is this. After that, the parameters for image quality utilized to store files are up to you. The following options are available to you when picking a high-quality setting:

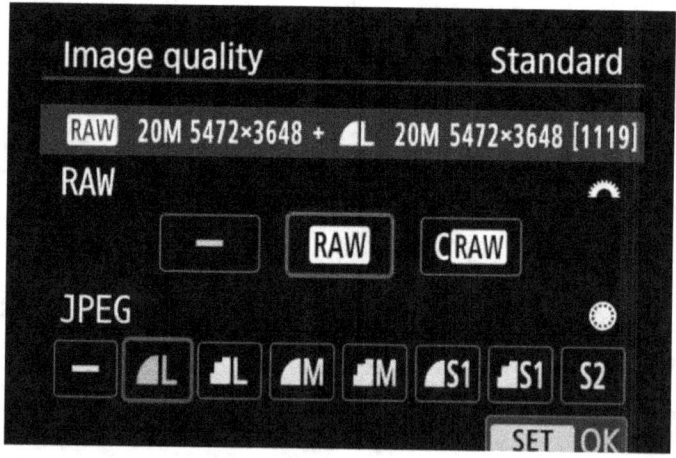

- **Resolution:** The absolute resolution of the images you take is based on the number of pixels captured. Among your options are: Large/RAW/C-RAW: 8192 × 5464 pixels (45MP); Medium: 5808 × 3872 pixels (22.5MP);

Small 1: 4176 × 2784 pixels (11.6MP); Small 2: 2400 × 1600 pixels (3.8MP)

- **JPEG/HEIF compression:** The camera utilizes compression to squish the images to a smaller size so that more photos may be saved on a specific memory card. Since this compacting slightly lowers the image quality, you can choose between Fine and Normal compression. The icons make it easier to recall that Normal compression (represented by a stair step icon) produces "jaggier" images. In contrast, Fine compression (represented by a quarter-circle) produces the smoothest results. The Small 2 (S2) file option is Fine quality but lacks a quality indicator. The distinction between JPEG and HEIF will be covered in the following section.

- **RAW, JPEG/HEIF, or both.** You can decide whether to save your shots as uncompressed, loss-free RAW files, which take up around four times as much space on your memory card, or JPEG/HEIF versions alone. Or you can shoot and simultaneously store both. To have a JPEG or HEIF version of the image that might be usable as-is as well as the original "digital negative" RAW file in case they wish to conduct some image processing in the future, many photographers choose to save both a JPEG and a RAW file. The result will be two distinct copies of the same image, one with a JPG extension and the other with the CR3 extension, which denotes a Canon RAW file.

Access the options, scroll to Image Quality, then press the SET button to select your desired combination. (If HDR recording is enabled in the Shooting 2 menu, HEIF will appear in the lower row in place of JPEG.)

To select among — (no RAW), RAW, or C RAW, spin the Main Dial. To choose a JPEGHEIF option, rotate the QCD-1: — (no JPEG/HEIF), Small 2 (with Fine compression), Large, Medium, or Small in Fine or Normal compression (represented by smooth and stepped icons, respectively). The choice that is presently selected has a red box around it. If you choose JPEG/HEIF Fine, it will be utilized for both RAW and JPEG/HEIF images. As always, press SET to confirm your choice after highlighting it.

WHY SO MANY OPTIONS? The Medium and Small resolution settings, Normal JPEG/HEIF compression settings, and the more compressed C-RAW format have limited advantages. They all enable extending the memory card's capacity, allowing you to cram many more photographs onto a single memory card. That can be helpful if you're traveling and running low on storage or shooting less-important material that doesn't require high resolution. Photos taken for real estate listings, website displays, photo ID cards, or other similar non-critical purposes can benefit from the Small 2 option.

Using higher compression and lower resolution for most work is frequently a false economy. You never know when you might require that additional image information. The best course of action is to stock up on memory cards so that you can photograph as much as you want to until you can transfer your pictures to a computer or other personal storage device.

As the camera can keep more images in its internal memory buffer before transferring them to the memory card, lower image quality can occasionally be advantageous if you take quick photo sequences. However, you'd probably prefer to take clearer, sharper photographs for most sports and other activities than to shoot continuously for longer.

Chapter 4: Reviewing Your Photos

Playback

You can access any of the features by tapping the icons or pressing the directional controls to move from one icon to the next. Then, when you've marked the adjustment you want to make, use the Main Dial or QCD-2, the directional controls, or both to choose from the available alternatives.

You have the following options:

- Protect images from accidental erasure. You can do this for individual photos or groups of pictures (but not from a card format).

- **Image rotation:** Rotate the visible image on display by 90 degrees at a time.

- **Rating:** Give photographs a star rating between one and five; you can sort and search for images according to each rating.

- **RAW image processing:** You can adjust a RAW image's brightness, white balance, picture style, auto lighting optimizer, high ISO noise reduction, image quality, color space, and lens aberration correction, among other RAW processing parameters. The original RAW file can then be saved with a processed JPEG version.

- **Resize:** Reduce the resolution of a full-frame Large image to Medium or Small.

- **Cropping:** You can alter an image's aspect ratio, straighten it, or all three, and then save the changed version.

- **Return:** Click this button to leave. Only the LCD screen version of the Quick Control menu has it. Both the LCD and Viewfinder screens' Q buttons can be used to depart.

- **Highlight alert:** Indicates whether or not highlight alerts are visible.

- **AF point display:** Displays the AF points used to take the photo.

- **Image jump:** During playback, hop between images using leaps of 1, 10, or a predetermined number of photos, by the date, the name of the folder, or by the parameters of movies, still images, protected images, or rated images.

- **Image search:** You can look for photographs using one or more search criteria, such as a specific rating, a particular date, a particular folder or protected state, or a specific type of file.

- **Transmit to smartphone:** Using this option, you can instantly send your photos to your smartphone and pick them up.

Enabling Automatic Picture Rotation

This function has an On/Off switch. When turned on, the LCD screen rotates vertically-oriented photos, so you don't have to swivel the camera to see them comfortably. However, this orientation also results in a smaller image because the image's longest dimension is displayed using the shortest dimension of the display. You've got three choices.

First, when using your picture-editing or viewing program, you can automatically rotate the image when seeing it in the camera and on your computer screen (this option is shown by a pair of camera/computer screen symbols). When evaluating your image in your image editor or viewing software, the image can be set to automatically rotate only once (just a computer screen icon is used). With this option, you can maximize the image on your camera's LCD while still having rotation applied when using your computer. Off is the third option. The image won't be rotated when viewed in the camera or on your computer. Note that if you switch Auto Rotate off, any pictures shot while the feature is disabled will not be automatically rotated when you turn Auto Rotate back on; information embedded in the image file when the photo is taken used to determine whether autorotation is applied.

Viewing Picture Data

File Information mode

A small amount of data, including the battery level, picture count, shutter speed, aperture, exposure compensation, ISO setting, the priority of the highlights in the image, and image quality, are displayed.

Highlight display mode

When you select Enable, overexposed highlight areas (often referred to as "blinkies") will blink on the LCD during image review. If this alert bothers you, set it to Disable. Many users access the histogram displays while the video is being played back as a more accurate gauge of overexposure (and underexposure).

Rating

Simply press the RATE button repeatedly while the video is playing to apply a rating to any photos or movies you've taken (or to use the rating system to reflect other criteria). Or, you can use this entry to disable the rating system or assign photos one, two, three, four, or five stars. Only photographs with the specified rating can be seen using the Image Jump feature. For example, imagine you were taking pictures of a track meet with numerous events. Jumping events might receive a one-star rating, relays a two-star rating, throwing events a three-star rating, hurdles a four-star rating, and dashes a five-star rating.

The Image Jump function would allow you only to view specific photographs. Use the ranking system for various categories if you use a little creativity. For example, you might categorize pictures taken at a wedding of the bride, the groom, visitors, ushers, and the couple's parents. If you were taking school pictures, the first grade might fall under one classification, the second under another, and so forth. This feature has far more applications than you might imagine if you give it a little attention. Additionally, ratings can be used to choose photographs in Digital Photo Professional or to designate images for a slideshow.

There are three ways to give a picture or movie a rating:

- **RATE button:** If the Playback 4 menu's Rate Button Function entry is selected, pushing the RATE button repeatedly will apply a rating from one to five stars, or none. You can limit ratings to just one to three stars, for example, by setting the number of stars in the Rate Button Function item.

- **Quick Control menu:** When you hit the Q button during Playback, the Quick Control menu that opens allows you to apply ratings as well. It is located in the left column, third from the top icon.

- **The menu option:** If you wish to swiftly apply ratings to more than a few images or movies, use the methods indicated below to apply a rating using this entry.

Simply take the following actions to use the Rating menu entry:

1. First, select the menu option for Rating.

2. To specify which images should be rated, select Select Images, Select Range, All Images in Folder, or All Images on Card.

3. When an image or movie you want to rate is visible, press SET, as previously mentioned under the Protect and Erase Images items; you can also choose a selection of images, all in a folder or all of those on a card.

4. Next, rotate the QCD-1 to assign a rating of one to five stars or to disable a rating. A maximum of 999 photos can be rated.

5. After the rating is complete, select MENU to leave.

Erase Images

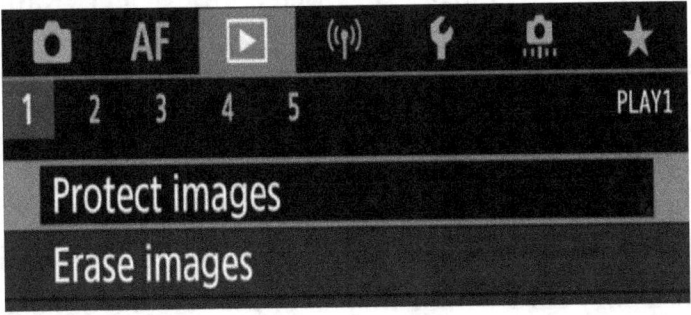

When selecting this menu item, you can select four options: Select Erase Images, Select Range, All Images in the Folder, and All Images on the Card. The first three options allow you to delete specific images, whereas the third option deletes all images on a card. Images that are protected won't be deleted.

However, using the Format command is frequently quicker and more comprehensive.

Similar in operation to the Protect function previously mentioned is this function. The default screen, which has these options, shows if no Image Search Conditions have been defined.

- **Choose and delete images:** Press the left/right directional controls to scroll through the photographs on your card. Next, press the SET button to designate an image for deletion or to remove a checkmark. Press the Q button when you're done choosing, and you'll be asked to confirm. To finish, select Cancel or OK and SET.

- **Select Range:** This option functions much like the range protects option. Selecting Select Range and pressing SET on the first photograph in a series can mark it. Then, after choosing the final image to be deleted, hit SET once more. To confirm and remove the pictures, press Q.

- **All Images in Folder:** A list of the folders on your memory card will be displayed. When you choose SET, a prompt asks you to confirm your choice and informs you that Protected photographs won't be deleted.

- **All Images on Card:** You'll be prompted to confirm this action. Except for the images you've tagged with the Protect command, the All Images on Card option deletes every image on the card.

If you have specified Image Search Conditions in the Playback 4 menu, your possibilities are as follows:

- **Choose and Remove Images:** Scroll through a collection of thumbnail previews to select any individual photographs on the current card.

- **Select Range:** As previously said, specify a continuous range of photographs on the card.

- **All Found Images:** Remove all photos discovered using the search criteria you specified in the Set Image Search Conditions field, excluding Protected images.

Memo Audio Quality

It permits the voice memos captured by the R5 to have their sampling rate customized. For example, professional video equipment, digital TV, DVD players, and other devices all employ a standard audio sampling rate of 48 kHz (kilo Hertz), which is what the High-Quality setting does. (MPEG 1 audio and consumer audio CDs commonly employ 44.1 kHz or 22 kHz.)

The 8 kHz sample rate used in the Low-Quality setting is comparable to that of a walkie-talkie, wireless intercom, and wireless microphone equipment. It is sufficient for human speech, but it might mute other noises. Clarity during playback should take priority, even for voice memos, even though high-quality recordings take up more space on your memory cards.

Protect Images

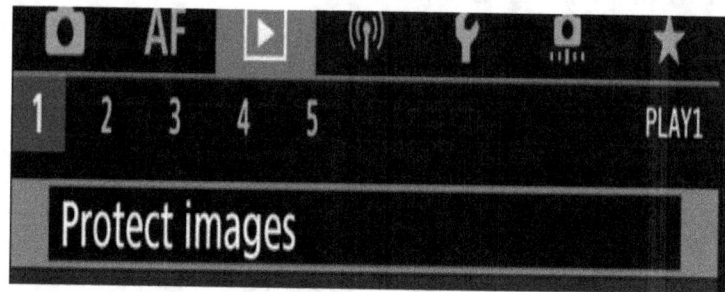

You can flag an image for protection if you don't want it to be unintentionally deleted using the Erase button or the Erase Images option in the Playback menu. Use this menu item or the Protect entry in the Quick Control menu's Playback section. When watching an image, hit the MENU button, then select Protect from the Playback 1 menu to protect one or more of the photos.

You'll see one of two screens:

- **Screen by default:** These options are shown on the default screen.

- **Select Images:** Select a specific image from the card shown by navigating a grid of thumbnail previews.

- **Select Range:** Choose the first image, press SET, scroll to the last picture, and press SET once more to choose a continuous range of photographs.

- **All Images in Folder:** Choose every picture in the folder. A list of accessible folders will be displayed for you (if more than one is available). To define the highlighted folder, press SET.

- **Unprotect All Images in Folder:** Choose a folder and turn off image protection for all of its images. Protect all of the photographs on the active card.

- **Unprotect All Images on the Card:** Unprotect every picture on the current card.

- **Specified Search screen**: You may instruct the camera to search for photographs using specific criteria while playback is in progress. Right appears if you have these search parameters set. Using these choices, you can then decide which photos to safeguard.

- **Select Images:** From a selection of thumbnail previews, select any of the individual images from the current card.

- **Select Range:** As previously said, specify a continuous range of photographs on the card.

- **All Found Photos:** Use the settings you selected in the Playback 4 menus Set Image Search Conditions box to protect all the images discovered. For instance, you may restrict access to only movies or still photos, images from a specific date, or pictures with a particular rating.

- **Unprotect All Found Photos:** Unprotect any images that match your image search criteria.

Cull Images Conveniently

You may quickly delete the "duds" from your memory card or just the ones in a specific folder with the help of the Protect feature. Just carry out these actions.

1. Give the RATE button the Protect function.

2. Depending on the extent of the culling you want, use the Protect feature as previously described to add protection to either All Images on Card or All Images in Folder.

3. Go through each image in Playback to review your collection.

4. Take down the shields. Press the RATE button to remove the protection when you see a photograph that isn't worth keeping.

5. Examine before erasing (optional). The best feature of this technique is that your card's photographs remain unchanged until you delete the clunkers. You can wait till a photography session is over, go back and look at your photos to see if your opinion has changed, or even copy everything from the card or folder to your computer (or to the second card you have inserted in the camera).

6. Use the Erase Images item to delete every image on a card or in a folder. The RATE button will only erase the

photographs that you made unprotected. The remaining items are secure.

7. Remove the final image protection (optional). You won't be able to delete the other pictures on your card later because they are all secured. Using Unprotect All Images in Folder or Unprotect All Images on Card, you can make them unprotected once again.

Chapter 5: Getting Creative with Exposure and Lighting

Introducing the Exposure Trio: Aperture, Shutter Speed, and ISO

Exposure is fundamentally a matter of light. Your photo's exposure may make or ruin it. By delivering the range of tones and colors required to generate the desired image, proper exposure brings out the detail in the regions you wish to photograph. Conversely, essential features may be obscured by poor exposure or lost in glare-filled, featureless stretches of white. Because digital sensors can't catch all the tones we can see, attaining the ideal exposure requires intelligence built into the camera or the intelligence in your thoughts.

When there is a wide range of tones in an image, including dazzling highlights and inky black shadows, we frequently have to choose an exposure that captures the majority of those tones—but not all—in the best way that best suits the image we are trying to create.

You're probably familiar with the conventional "exposure triangle," which consists of the ISO sensitivity of the sensor, shutter speed, and aperture (the amount of light and light passing through the lens with each other to form an exposure).

The amount of light that is available has an impact on the trio as a whole. Therefore, you may get twice as much exposure by doubling the amount of light, widening the aperture by one stop, lengthening the shutter speed by two times, or increasing the ISO setting by two times. To maintain the same exposure, you can also improve one of these elements while decreasing another by a comparable amount.

Any of the three controls requires trade-offs when used. Smaller f/stops improve depth of field while larger f/stops provide less depth of field (and potentially, at the same time, can decrease sharpness through a phenomenon called diffraction). Longer shutter speeds increase the likelihood of motion blur, whereas shorter shutter speeds do a better to eliminate the impact of camera/subject motion. While lower ISO settings lessen the effects of noise, higher ISO settings increase the amount of visual noise and artifacts in your image.

Exposure affects how a picture looks, feels, and sounds. Even the best-composed photograph might need to be properly exposed since it can drown out key tones in darkness or make them appear featureless to the eye. On the other hand, the right exposure brings out the detail in the regions you want to photograph and offers the variety of tones and colors you need to get the image you want. Because digital sensors can't record all the tones we can perceive, achieving the ideal exposure can be challenging. The sensor might be unable to record every tone in an image if there is a wide range of tones, including dazzling highlights and inky black shadows. Sometimes we have to make do with an exposure that captures the majority of those tones—but not all—in a way that works best for the image we're trying to capture. To capture the tones that matter in your photograph, you'll frequently need to decide which aspects are crucial and which are not. That is a component of the creativity you use to execute your photographic vision. In addition, the dynamic range of digital camera sensors is constrained, making it difficult to capture detail in both highlights and shadows in a single image.

Exploring the Advanced Exposure Modes

You can specify exposure manually, pick entirely automatic exposure, or select a shutter speed or aperture setting that you prefer for artistic reasons. The system automatically chooses an ISO speed for you in any situation, typically staying within the ISO 100–12,800 range. Various exposure mode and ISO speed setting combinations chosen in the Shooting 2 menu may result in some bizarre exceptions. The AF-point selection button is to the right of the * button, and it can be used to unlock exposure and unlock it again.

A wide variety of exposure changes are available with the R5. Following are your choices:

- **Fully automatic exposure:** If Scene Intelligent Auto, P, or B is chosen as the mode, the camera will choose the proper exposure for you automatically (bulb exposure). Be aware that using the B position will not result in a bulb or time exposure; instead, the camera will default to P. The goal is to stop you from unintentionally selecting B and losing your ability to record video. The upper-left corner of the LCD monitor will show the scene type that the camera has chosen after analyzing your subject in Scene Intelligent Auto.

- **Shutter-priority AE:** With some restrictions, you can select Tv just like you would when taking still photos and then define a shutter speed. The camera will determine your aperture. Because you can't (logically) select a shutter speed that is longer than the amount of time required to expose a single picture, the shutter speeds that are accessible will depend on the frame rate. For instance, you cannot utilize a shutter speed greater than 130th seconds at 30/25/24 fps. The maximum shutter speed at 60/50 frames per second is 1/60th second. Shutter speeds less than 1/4000th second (1/8,000th) are invariably not accessible.

Self-determining the shutter speed has two benefits. First, even though each frame is only recorded for between 1/60 and 1/30 of a second, reducing the amount of time the sensor is exposed to light enables video recording in a significantly wider variety of lighting situations.

For example, even with a very narrow f/stop and an ISO 100 sensitivity level, 1/30th second would result in overexposure when taken outside in broad daylight. Also, choosing a faster shutter speed lets you stop moving with each shot, minimizing or eliminating blur. When filming sports, choose 1/500th second, and if you want to add a little motion blur for emphasis, keep with 1/30th second.

- **Aperture-priority AE:** Choose Av, then you can select a f/stop to either increase or decrease the depth of field for artistic effects. Your choice of f/stop has no restrictions. However, you should avoid changing the aperture while recording video because the abrupt change may have an unsettling effect.

- **Manual exposure:** Select M and enter the ISO, shutter, and aperture values.
    - **ISO:** To access the ISO speed setting screen, press the ISO/Flash Exposure Compensation button on top of the camera. Utilize the Main Dial to adjust. Selecting Auto will cause the camera to choose the proper ISO based on your shutter speed and aperture. If you choose Auto, the * button during Manual exposure locks the ISO at the current level.
    - **Shutter speed:** Within the constraints outlined under Shutter-priority AE earlier, choose a shutter speed using the Main Dial.
    - **Aperture:** Change the aperture with Quick Control Dial 1.

The exposure level scale at the bottom of the LCD screen allows you to check exposure when selecting shutter speed or aperture. In addition, you can examine a live histogram by clicking the INFO button for an additional check.

Setting ISO, Aperture, and Shutter Speed

Adjusting aperture

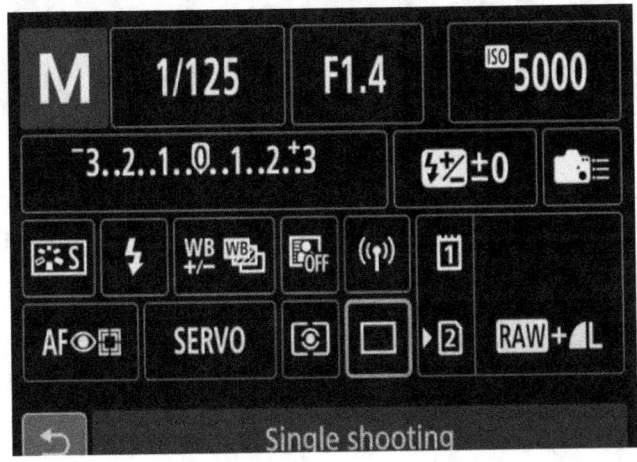

You can specify an aperture range with this item. You can manually adjust the aperture within the range you choose when using the Av, M, and Bulb exposure modes.

When taking still pictures in P and Tv, the aperture will be set automatically within this range. The maximum apertures of f/1.0 to f/64 and minimum apertures (the smallest f/stops) of f/91 to f/1.4 can be selected. Naturally, these "limits" are based on maximum and minimum apertures. Use this input to reduce the number of f-stops available, such as to maintain selective focus or, in the other direction, to increase depth-of-field (even if it costs you some sharpness because of diffraction).

Adjusting shutter speed

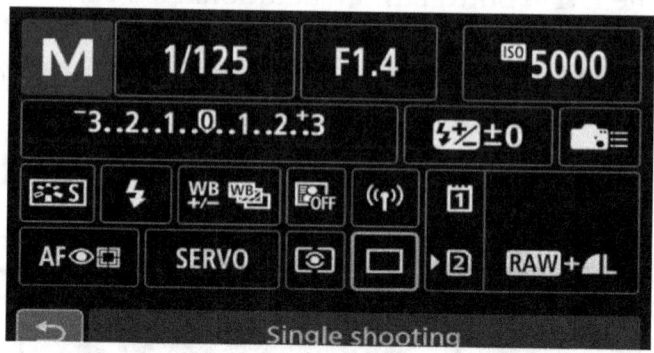

When utilizing Tv or M exposure modes, or the value the camera chooses automatically in P and Av modes, there are situations when you want to limit the shutter speed range. For instance, you might want to lock off any shutter speeds more than 1/500th second if you're photographing motor sports and want to keep a little blur in the tires of the cars (to avoid the "frozen in time" appearance" look").

When the upper limit is reached, you might not care whether your aperture changes, or you might let Auto ISO start to drop the sensitivity by one or two notches to allow for the best exposure. On the other hand, if you know that 1/60th second is the shortest shutter speed at which a hand-held image will be acceptably sharp, you should avoid using shutter speeds lower than that. Depending on your creative requirements, you can choose a "top" shutter speed from 1/8000th second to 15 seconds and a "bottom" speed from 30 seconds to 14000th second.

Controlling ISO

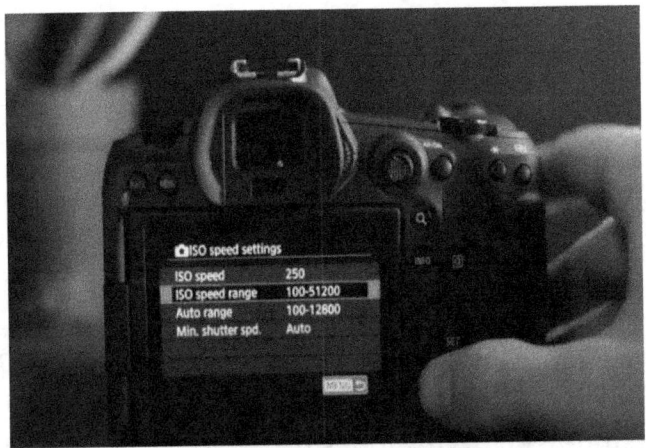

Using the M-Fn button on top of the camera is the most straightforward method of changing ISO sensitivity. Without first clicking the AF point selection button, you can push it to bring up a screen with several settings. To select the setting that will be changed, turn either Quick Control Dial. The one that is furthest to the left is ISO. Next, rotate the Main Dial to cycle between the available ISO settings, ranging from ISO Auto to ISO 100 to ISO 102,400, when it is highlighted. To confirm, press SET.

Choosing an Exposure Metering Mode

The next setting you should change is metering mode. Note that the camera must be in one of the manual or semiautomatic modes, not Scene Intelligent Auto (A+), for this setting and the ones that follow. The default Evaluative metering is generally the most excellent option as you learn to know your camera among the four metering settings I'll discuss next. Use the Quick Control screen to switch between metering modes. It has several variations and can be accessed in one of the following three ways:

Option 1: While using the viewfinder, say:

- Press the Q button to access the Quick Control screen for the camera's viewfinder.

- To access the Metering Mode icon, the sixth from the top in the left column, rotate the QCD-1. Then choose one of the following four modes by rotating the Main Dial.

  To confirm, press SET.

Option 2: As you gaze at the LCD:

- The screen will either provide a graphic-based information screen or one of many photographic previews of your subject. (By pushing the INFO button, you can switch between various informational displays.)

- If the image preview is visible, click the Q button and, using the directional controls as indicated in Option 1 above, choose a metering mode from the LCD version of the Quick Control screen that appears. The main distinction is that the options are surrounded by boxes, indicating that you can tap them using the touch screen rather than using navigational controls, which you can do for Option 3, discussed below.

- Press the Q button to view the Quick Control panel in the graphic form if the graphic screen is not already visible.

Next, locate the Metering Mode symbol in the bottom row of icons in the center. To select a mode, turn either dial, then press SET to confirm.

Option 3: Access either the LCD or graphic versions of the Quick Control screen when using touch controls, as explained in Option 2.

- On either screen, tap the Metering Mode icon and the desired metering mode. Then, you can confirm and leave by tapping the "Return" arrow icon.

Applying Exposure Compensation

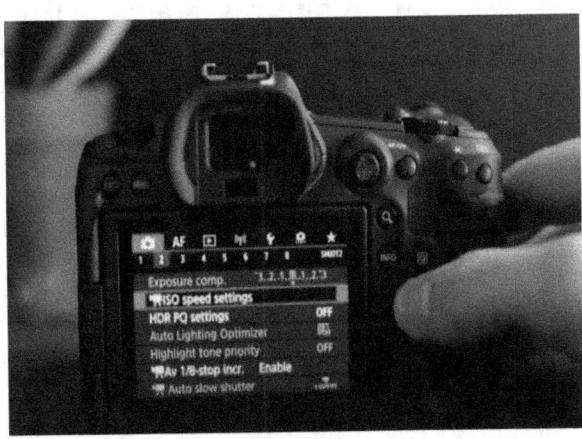

Expo. Comp./AEB, also known as exposure compensation and automatic exposure bracketing, is the first option under the Shooting 2 menu. Compared to the metered value, exposure compensation either increases or decreases exposure. You can adjust it from this screen or simply press the shutter release halfway and spin the QCD-1 to add or subtract exposure in Fv,

P, Tv, or AV modes. While compensation is active, a plus/minus exposure compensation indication scale is shown.

Shooting multiple consecutive exposures with various settings while using the AEB feature increases the likelihood that one will be right. When you combine numerous images to make a high dynamic range (HDR) image, automatic exposure bracketing is a great approach to get the basic exposures you'll need.

When this menu option is chosen, automatic exposure bracketing will be activated. To define the range that the bracket will cover, which can be up to plus/minus three stops from the base exposure, rotate the Main Dial to expand or contract the three lines below the scale. Then, spin the bracket set left or right using the QCD-1 (or Multicontroller joystick) to change the base exposure point from the metered (0) value and bias the bracketing toward underexposure (rotate left) or overexposure (rotate right) (rotate right).

The bracketed shots will be exposed when AEB is turned on in the following order: metered exposure decreased exposure, and increased exposure.

Tonal Range

The range of dark to light tones can be adjusted with histograms, from the absence of any brightness (black) to the brightest tone that is feasible (white) and all the middle tones in between. So even though you're capturing those tones in three distinct color layers of red, green, and blue, it's easier to think of a photo's tonality in terms of a black-and-white or grayscale image because all values for tones fall within a continuous range between black and white.

The tonal "spectrum" in your photographs isn't continuous because they are digital; instead, it is broken up into discrete steps that stand in for the various tones that can be recorded. There are 20 gray steps total, ranging from 100 percent gray (black) on the left to 0 percent gray (white) on the right (plus white).

The digital values from 0 to 255 that your sensor recorded for an image with 8 bits per channel run the length of the chart's bottom. A 24-bit, a full-color image is created by combining 8 bits of red, 8 bits of green, and 8 bits of blue. Any caught black would have a value of 0, the brightest white would have a value of 255, and the mid-tones would be grouped around the 128 markers. When the camera is set to 14 bits per channel for a RAW file, the recorded information may be "finer" and range from 0 to 4,094.

Grayscale photographs, also called black-and-white photography, are simple to comprehend. At least, that is what we believe. A black-and-white photograph gives the impression that there is a continuous spectrum of tones from black to white, along with all the grays in between. But that could be more accurate. Any photograph's deepest black is never genuinely black since light is always reflected from the print's surface. When viewed on a screen, the deepest black is only as dark as what a computer monitor can produce. Even the lightest areas of a print absorb some light (only a mirror reflects nearly all the light that strikes it), and when viewing on a computer monitor, the whites are only as bright as the display's LCD or LED picture components. As a result, even the whitest white isn't a true white. That continuous set of tones doesn't encompass the entire grayscale tonal range because there aren't any darker blacks or brighter, whiter whites.

When an image has broad sections of shades that gradually transition from one level to another, such as areas of sky, water, or walls, the complete range of tones becomes relevant. Imagine a photograph of a camping party gathered around a fire. There aren't many shadows on the campers' faces because the fire's light is straight in their faces. All the hues that make up the characteristics of the individuals gathered around the fire are condensed into the lighter end of the brightness range.

But this scene is more than just faces. Trees, rocks, and perhaps a few creatures that have risen from the shadows to investigate the situation are behind the campers. The softer light that reflects off the surrounding surfaces shines on these. You'll notice a ton of detail in these shadow photographs after your eyes adjust to the dim lighting.

In any case, it would be impossible to recreate this campfire setting faithfully. A high-contrast lighting condition is probably already making you cringe if you are an experienced photographer. When there are fewer tones, and they are all grouped at a few specific scale points, certain photographs may have strong contrast. Although there are more tones in a low-contrast image, they are dispersed so thinly that the picture appears flat. You can use a histogram on your digital camera to see how these tones relate to one another.

Chapter 6: Downloading, Organizing, and Archiving Your Picture Files

Sending Pictures to the Computer

Connecting the camera and computer

Using a USB cable, transmit pictures from the camera to a Mac or PC as follows:

1. Disconnect the camera.

2. Remove the camera's USB port cover and insert the Type-C cable included in the package into the USB port.

3. Join the USB cable's other end to your computer's USB Type-C port. (If your device doesn't have a USB Type-C connector, you might need to utilize an extra Type-C-to-USB-A converter.)

4. Switch the camera on. Either the camera shows up on your desktop as a mass storage device, allowing you to drag and drop the images to your computer, or your installed program often identifies the camera and offers to transfer the pictures.

Starting the transfer process

To use a card reader to transfer pictures from a memory card to a computer:

1. Disconnect the camera.

2. Slide open the memory card door, press the memory card, and it will pop up so you can remove it.

3. Place the memory card in the reader for your memory card. The files on the card are recognized by your installed software, which then offers to transfer them. In addition, you can open the card's desktop appearance to reveal a mass storage device, which you can use to drag and drop data onto your computer.

Downloading and Organizing Photos with the Canon Software

Downloading with Canon Transfer

1. To connect the camera to the PC, use any USB Type-C cable.

2. Ensure that the camera is connected to the images or movies' memory card.

3. Activate the camera.

4. To download photos and videos to your Mac or PC, use the EOS Utility. EOS Utility is a program that Canon makes available without charge. It's crucial to understand that programs like Image Capture (on the Mac) won't function accurately when transferring pictures and videos from the Canon R5. Unlike many

other cameras, the Canon R5 won't appear in the Finder on your Mac or in your file folder on your PC. That's unfortunate because, like with many other cameras, it's convenient to drag and drop or copy and paste files from the camera into your PC or Mac.

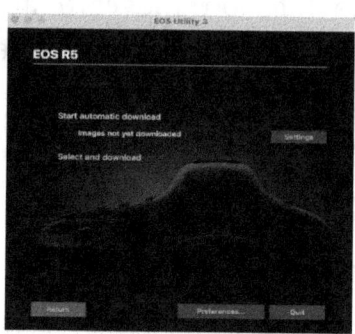

5. Once the EOS Utility appears on your screen, select Preferences. Then, go to your applications and launch the software directly if the EOS Utility doesn't appear on your screen.

6. Select the target folder from the drop-down option at the top dialogue boxes. Next, choose the Mac or PC folder where you wish the pictures or videos to be saved.

7. Return to the EOS Utility's main screen and select Download Images to Computer.

8. You can then start the automatic download or make any other changes.

Browsing images with the Main Dial

Depending on the jump technique selected, you can move the Main dial to forward or rewind the images in a single-image display.

1. Select Image jump.

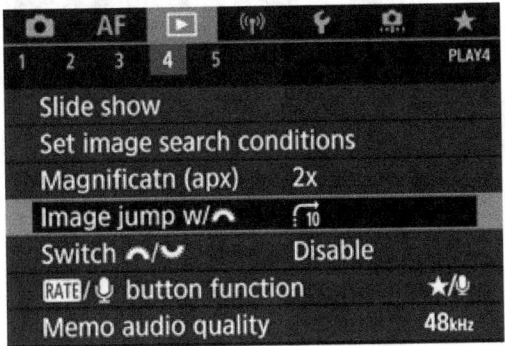

2. Select the jump method.

Note

- You can choose the number of images to jump by turning the Main dial to the [Jump images by the given number] setting.

- Turn the Main dial to choose the rating for [Display by image rating] (). As you browse, all rated photographs will be displayed if you select Rating.

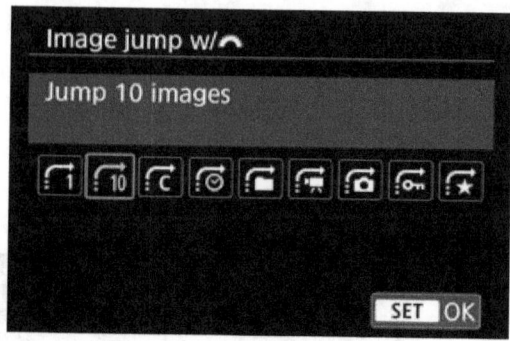

3. Browse by jumping.

   (1) Jump method

   (2) Playback position

   - Press the Playback button.

   - In the single-image display, turn the Main dial.

   You can browse by the jump method set.

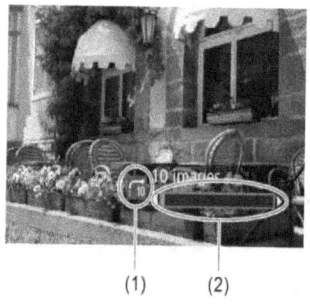

(1)   (2)

Organizing pictures

Moving Images

To arrange photos by the date of the shot or theme, you can move or copy them to a different folder.

Drag images of moving or copy them.

- To move: Drag images to the destination folder.

- To copy: Drag images to the destination folder while holding down the Ctrl key (Windows) or Option key (macOS).

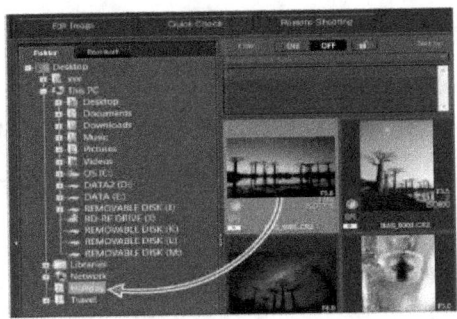

Moving Images by Folder

To arrange photographs into folders, you can move or copy the folders.

Move or copy folders by dragging them.

- **To move:** Drag folders to the destination folder.

- **To copy:** Holding down the Ctrl (Windows) or Option key while dragging folders to the desired folder (macOS).

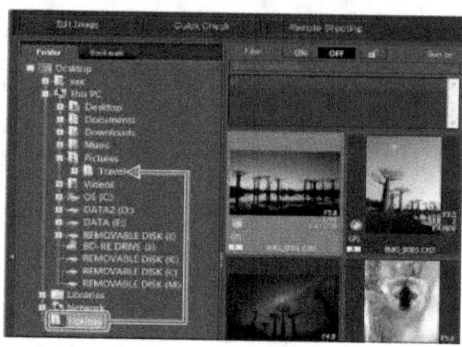

Processing RAW Files

RAW Processing (RAW/DPRAW)

It is the first item at the top of the Playback 3 menu page. RAW Processing (RAW/DPRAW) is the entry's label, and it can operate on Dual Pixel RAW files in addition to regular RAW files.

With this option, you can instantly create JPEG or HEIF copies of your full-size RAW photographs (but not S RAW files). No changes are made to the original RAW image. Only suitable RAW (or RAW and DPRAW with the R5) photographs are available when you choose this menu entry. Just carry out these actions.

1. **View RAW images:** On the first screen, click Select Images or Select Range to select specific RAW images (to choose a continuous series of images). Then, to browse through compatible photos, rotate the QCD-1. Instead, several index photos will be activated when you press the

Magnify button and turn the Main Dial in the opposite direction.

2. **Choose the image to be processed:** To choose the image to be processed, press SET. There will be a checkmark next to it. Press the Q button to proceed to the next step after selecting.

3. **Use Shot Settings or Set Up Processing (JPEG or HEIF):** If you choose Use Shot Settings on the following screen, the camera will immediately produce JPEG copies of the RAW image(s) you selected before requesting your permission to save as a brand-new file. Step 4 is where you should go if you wish to change the settings.

   Note: If you choose the default Use Shot Settings option. JPEGs are produced if HDR PQ Settings are set to Disable; HEIFs are produced if they are set to Enable.

4. **Set the parameters:** A screen with a list of parameters you can change appears. Use the Multi-controller joystick to navigate to the parameter you want to change. Among your options are the following:

   - Changing the brightness
   - The White Balance
   - Image Format (A, 1, 2, and 3 Styles with JPEG only)

- Precision (JPEG only)

- Face Lighting + Auto Lighting Optimizer (JPEG only).

- Noise Reduction at High ISO

- Clarity of the image, color space, and lens aberration correction

5. **Make changes:** All settings will already be as they were when the RAW file was exposed. Then, rotate either the Main Dial or QCD-1 to choose an option when the parameter you want to change is highlighted. Next, press the Magnify button to expand a section of the image for evaluation because specific changes are challenging to see. To confirm your selection and return to the main screen, press SET.

6. Repetition of Step 5 is optional. You can keep modifying any or all of the other parameters. In addition, you can undo all of your previous modifications at any time by pressing the Trash/Erase button.

7. Compare the old and new: this is the fun part. You can compare your before-and-after photographs by pressing the INFO button after you've made your edits. The parameters you changed will be highlighted in orange in the screen's upper-right corner when the image is displayed in the After Change version (and is identified as such). To switch between the After Change and Shot

Settings (original) versions, rotate the QCD-1. (Effects of the Digital Lens Optimizer are only visible in the enlarged view.) To exit Compare mode, press MENU.

8. Save JPEG/HEIF: After making your desired changes, select the Save icon at the bottom right of the screen (near the Return arrow), and then press SET. Selecting OK will create a new file; selecting Cancel will stop the procedure. If the original image was captured with a different aspect ratio than 3:2, it will appear in those proportions and be saved as a JPEG or HEIF file.

9. Go on with the procedure? If you've chosen many photographs, you'll be prompted to decide if you want to keep processing them. Select Yes to proceed.

10. Choose which image to display: You can instruct the camera to show the Original Image or the Processed Image.

11. Repeat. Continue processing all the photographs you want to use if you have additional images selected.

DPRAW Processing

You could use this entry to apply portrait relighting using a virtual light source and modify background clarity if you took your photo using the DPRAW option. The RAW Processing (RAW/DPRAW) works similarly, and you can choose DPRAW photographs to work with.

You'll get presented with a screen that lets you select between Portrait Relighting or Background Clarity when you reach this menu option. To proceed, press SET. The option you selected will now appear as a new icon next to the Auto Lighting Optimizer icon. As you look at the image you're editing,

- **Portrait Relighting:** Place the light source using the Multi-controller joystick. The light source is in front when the white and black dots cross. To switch from Low to Standard to High light intention. Use the Magnify button to switch from Spot to Medium to Wide light coverage. If more than one face is shown (up to 10 faces may be recognized), tap the touch screen or rotate the QCD-1 while holding down the RATE button to choose another. For comparison, the INFO button and QCD-1 alternate between After Change and Before Change. To save, press SET.

    Notes: Only JPEG photos can be produced; HEIF files cannot. Background Clarity and Portrait Relighting cannot be used on the same image. Images are always shown horizontally, even if they were taken in a vertical orientation.

- **Background Clarity:** You can change blurry backgrounds on a scale from -4 to +4, judging the changes as you examine an image on the screen. Make adjustments using the Main Dial or QCD-1, and then press SET to confirm. You may view the After Change and Shot Settings versions using the INFO button and

QCD-1. Items that have been edited will have an orange highlight.

When working with subjects that include nearby bright or dark areas, Background Clarity may cause evident fringing. In addition, this function may impact places other than the background in photographs with a noticeable background blur.

Chapter 7: Capturing Video

Getting Started

Even if you are in any still shooting mode, shooting movies on the spot is simple. All you have to do with the R5 is push the Movie button (located on top of the camera to the southwest of the shutter release and marked with a red dot). Press the button one more to end the shooting. All there is to it is that. When you choose Scene Intelligent Auto as your movie mode, the camera tries to determine what kind of scene is being taken and places an icon for that scene in the upper-left corner of the screen.

There are numerous potential icons. The background (bright, bright/backlit, blue sky, blue sky/backlit, sunset, spotlight, and dark) and the subject (people, people in motion, nature/outdoors, in motion, and close-up) are taken into consideration while choosing a scene. To help brighten the background, the camera can also recognize when it is mounted on a tripod and switch scene modes with slower shutter rates. While Scene Intelligent Auto is suitable for occasional usage, you should switch to one of the "official" movie modes if you require the most excellent flexibility and total control over your settings. When in movie mode, the R5 starts filming in one of two ways.

R5 Video Overview

The R5 does not have a mode dial. You should be able to switch between the various modes on the camera by using the MODE button and displays. Just carry out these actions.

1. **Press the MODE button:** The selection screen that shows your options will appear after you press the MODE button.

2. **Enter Movie mode:** To enter Movie mode while still shooting mode, you must press the INFO button. Scene Intelligent Auto (A+), Program AE, Shutter-priority, Aperture-priority, and Manual Exposure are the settings in the top row, going from left to right.

3. **Change exposure:** The camera will adjust your exposure in Scene Intelligent Auto and Program AE mode. You can set the shutter speed or aperture by choosing the Tv or Av modes. Both options are selectable in M mode. The three Custom shooting movie modes— C1, C2, and C3—are in the bottom row.

4. **Concentrate on your subject:** You should focus manually or automatically. Movie Servo AF is on by default. To focus using the current AF technique, halfway press the shutter button.

5. Go back. When finished, use the Return arrow to leave.

6. To begin or stop recording, tap the red dot in the screen's upper-right corner or press the Movie Shooting button by again pushing the button or tapping the dot. The type

and quantity of information presented can be changed by pressing the INFO button, just like screens for still photos.

Movie Recording Quality

Additional video recording choices on your camera include 8K and incredibly high-resolution 4K footage with the R5. In addition, the following options are available to you.

- **The movie recording's size:** The movie has resolutions of 8K (R5 only), 4K, and Full HD. The resolution and film area varies depending on the recording quality and movie crop settings. Using the terms 8K-D/4K-D and 8K-U/4K-U, the R5 distinguishes between television and movie aspect ratios (proportions).

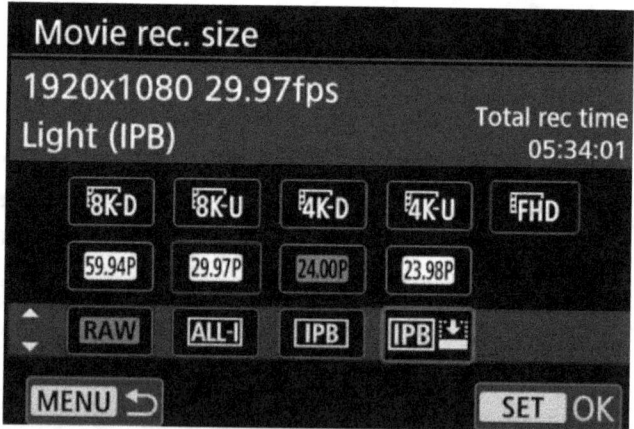

Remarks: The 4K HQ (High Quality) mode on the R5 enables the 4K-D Fine and 4K-U Fine modes, which have frame rates of 29.97P, 24.00P, and 23.98P with options for All-I, IPB, and IPB Lite compression.

- **High Frame Rate** refers to the number of discrete frames or fields captured per second. These are commonly represented as 120, 60, 30, and 24 frames per second in NTSC mode, which is used in North America, Japan, and other countries; frame rates (100, 50, and 25) differ in Europe and other territories using the PAL specification. As I'll explain below, the actual frames-per-second is slightly lower than the stated value.

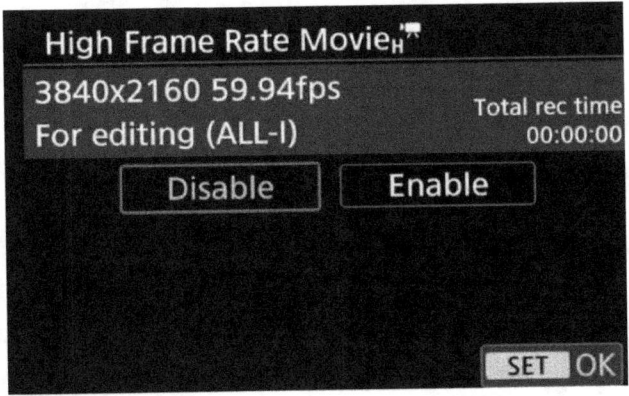

It should be noted that when you scroll to enable high frame rate videos, your video is recorded in resolutions of 119.9P (NTSC) or 100.0P (PAL) but is played back at speeds of 29.97/25.00 fps, creating 4X slow motion (one second of the action takes four seconds to playback.) However, if you output video from the camera through the HDMI connector, it will be displayed in a 2X slow-motion format. It is because the R5 captures High Frame

Rate movies in 4K and Full HD with ALL-I compression and exclusively in Full HD with IPB compression.

The maximum length of a clip is 7 minutes and 29 seconds, and it cannot have sound. Time codes are not recorded when Count Up is set to Free Run (as described later). The flickering was visible under fluorescent or LED lighting.

- **Compression Technique:** To save storage space and ease the burden on the transmission rates of the gathered frames to your storage device, each frame is compressed using either the ALL-I or IPB formats. IPB and All-I are both used by the R5. In addition, "IPB Lite" versions for the R5 employ reduced bit-rate capture; these versions can be recognized by an icon with an arrow pointing down.

Except for RAW (R5 only), all movies are stored using the MP4 format as the "container" for your video files and the MPEG4 AVC/H.264 codec (coder-decoder). MP4, an international standard that will be briefly described, supports and uses progressive scans. RAW files for the R5 have a .CRM extension, while MP4 files have a .MP4 extension. Owners of the R5 can choose between recording in MP4 and RAW+MP4.

Movie Cropping

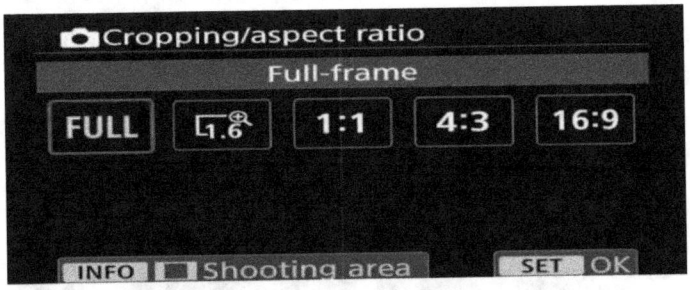

When filming movies, the actual region of the sensor's full image size that is captured is always cropped to some degree. A portion of your frame is cropped off the top and bottom because FHD, 4K, and 8K aspect ratios are 16:9 rather than the 3:2 ratio utilized for still photography.

The remaining area may be further cropped depending on your lenses and the video mode, the remaining area may be further cropped. You have some control over the image crop by using this parameter. I'll describe the different croppings utilized for the R5.

- **Movie Cropping:** Using an adapter, you can utilize this mode with RFmount and EF-mount lenses (typical full-frame lenses).

- **Movie Cropping:** When selecting this option, your movie is always cropped, and the resulting image area matches Canon APS-C lenses with the EF-S prefix.

  Note: The R5 cannot capture High Frame Rate videos using EF-S lenses or Movie Cropping enabled. When utilizing Movie, Digital IS, a small additional crop is applied. When using the R5, EF-S lenses cannot be placed on the camera, and 8K and 4K videos cannot be recorded.

Movie Self-timer

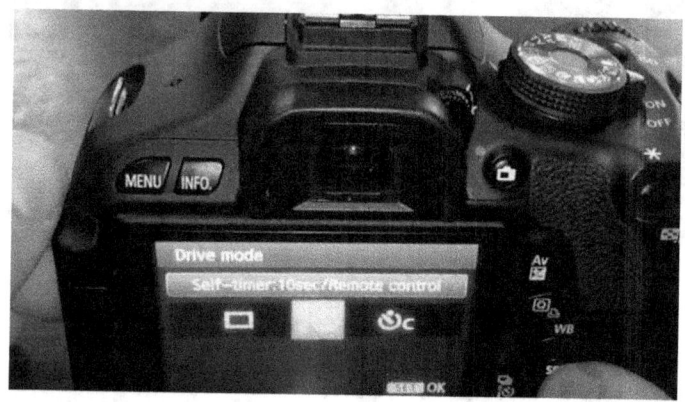

It is the menu item that appears initially in Movie Shooting 6. This useful function chooses whether to delay the start of movie capture for 10 or 2 seconds. It allows you to prepare yourself for the camera (choose 10 seconds if you need to comb your hair; pick 2 seconds if you're designed to go or don't care). This setting can also allow the camera to stabilize itself after you've jabbed the Movie button with your index finger if you don't have a remote release. Don't stab people!

Vloggers could also use this capability for an unplanned session. Still, they probably wouldn't need to because those who use an R5 (instead of a smartphone) are also skilled at editing tools to cut out the scene's annoying rush.

Remote Control

You must allow your camera to start/stop recording movies using a remote control. The Remote Controller RC-6 and Wireless Remote Control BR-E1 are compatible with the R5. In addition, the wired Remote Switch RS-80N3/TC-80N3 is compatible with the R5. Learn about the features of each device by consulting the instructions with your remote.

IS (Image Stabilizer Mode)

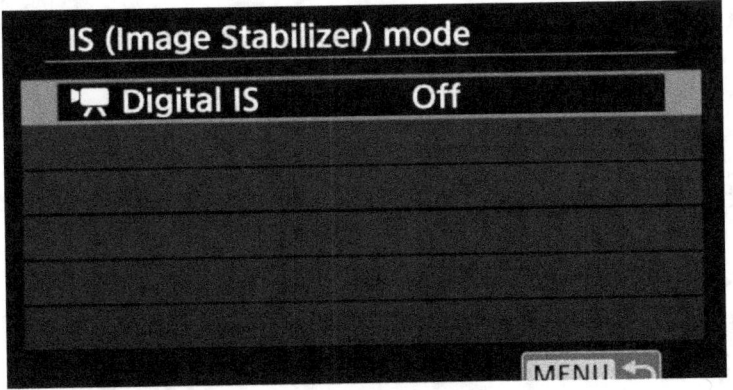

The Movie Shooting 7 menu begins with this option. Although your camera depends on the optical image stabilization (OIS) incorporated into some RF- and EF/EF-S mount lenses, it may also use an electronic form of OIS called Movie Digital IS that can be turned on when recording video.

Digital image stabilization uses the fact that video frames that have been cropped still retain some image data outside the actual frame being presented. The camera can detect movement and correct for it by slowly altering all of the frame's pixels, keeping stationary subjects in the exact relative location within the frame. In other words, if there is a slight movement of the camera picture to the left by a few pixels, the frame area is also shifted by an equal number of pixels to the right.

As a result, the produced movie is somewhat cropped, adding a minor amount of magnification, as some pixels at the frame's edges must be removed to make up for this adjustment. Additional cropping magnification is used when using EF-S lenses or if the Movie Cropping function is chosen.

You must use this feature with your lenses' built-in optical image stabilization to be effective (if your lens has IS but is off, this feature won't function). A list of lenses compatible with what Canon refers to as "combination IS" is provided (when both digital and optical image stabilization are combined).

You cannot use the movie IS with lenses up to 800mm; it is not advised to use it with third-party, tilt/shift (TS-E), or fisheye lenses. You have the following choices:

- **Off:** Digital IS is not used. However, when the camera is mounted to a tripod.

- **On:** The image will be gently cropped, giving the appearance of being somewhat magnified, and a significant camera shake will be rectified. Wide-angle lenses perform best with this setting.

- **Enhanced:** The image will be enlarged to account for an even more pronounced camera shake. The image may appear noticeably blurry while watching, and there may be an increase in visual noise, so use this as a last resort.

Zebra Setting

This feature warns you when highlight levels in your image are brighter than a setting you specify in this menu option. It's somewhat comparable to the flashing "blinkies" that digital cameras have long used during image review to tell us, after the fact, which highlight areas of the image we just took are blown out.

Zebra patterns are a much more useful tool because you are given an alert before you take the picture and can specify precisely how bright too bright it is. The Zebra feature has been a staple of professional video shooting for a long time, as you might guess from the moniker assigned to the unit used to specify brightness: IRE, a measure of video signal level, which stands for Institute of Radio Engineers.

When you want to use Zebra pattern warnings, access this menu entry, choose your pattern and specify an IRE brightness value from 5 to 100 (depending on the pattern selected). Once you see the results on your display, you can adjust your exposure settings to reduce the brightness of the highlights.

So, exactly how bright is too bright? A value of 100 IRE indicates pure white, so any Zebra pattern visible when using this setting means that your image is extremely overexposed. Any details in the highlights are gone and cannot be retrieved.

You can use settings from 70 to 90 to ensure facial tones are not overexposed.

Generally, Caucasian skin falls in the 80 IRE range, with darker skin tones registering as low as 70 and very fair skin or lighter areas of your subject edging closer to 90 IRE. Once you've decided on the approximate range of tones you want to ensure it does not blow out, you can set the camera's Zebra pattern sensitivity appropriately and receive the flashing striped warning on your display. The pattern does not appear in your final image—it's just an aid to keep you from blowing it. Maximum brightness value can vary, depending on your Canon Log, Highlight Tone Priority, Picture Style, and HDRPQ settings.

Your adjustment options for the zebra setting include:

- **Zebra:** Choose On or Off to enable/disable the display of Zebra patterns during movie shooting.

- **Zebra Pattern:** There are two Zebra patterns to choose from right-slanting diagonal lines. These appear over areas that exceed your specified brightness level. You can also elect to show Zebra 1+2, an overlapping pattern where the two warnings merge. That allows you to see areas representing a combination of the two levels.

- **Zebra 1 Level:** You can set the Zebra 1 display from 5 to 95 percent (with plus/minus 5 percent tolerance).

- **Zebra 2 Level:** The Zebra 2 level can be specified from 50 to 100 percent.

Overheat Control

The Movie Shooting 8 menu begins with this option. While you preview or record video, the sensor is powered on, and memory card storage is constantly in use. Other features like exposure metering and autofocus are also working diligently. Unfortunately, heat is produced in large amounts when shooting 4K and 8K footage at high speeds and rapid transmission rates. This Overheat control aids in preventing the camera from overheating and potentially harming the sensor while it is on standby. If none worries you, you can change the default setting of On to Off. Your main benefit is a quicker response time when you resume capture and a better standby screen display.

Movie Autofocus Menus

A new set of four Movie Autofocus menus with a total of 17 entries display once you've selected one of the movie shooting modes. Instead, I'll discuss the three new entries and explain the distinctions that pertain to autofocus when filming movies. Of course, you will get accustomed to your other movie AF options, such as AF Method, from still photography. The first difference is the menu:

- **AF 1 Menu:** The Still and Movie versions of the AF 1 menus are nearly identical, except that the Movie version does not include Continuous AF or AF Operation (One-Shot/Servo option). One new entry has been added, and I'll talk about it shortly: Movie Servo AF.

The only difference between the Still and Movie versions of the AF 2 menu is that the Movie version does not have an entry for AF-Assist Beam Firing.

- **AF 3 Menu:** In Movie mode, the items in the AF 4 menu for still photography have taken the Still photo AF 3 menu position. The Orientation Linked AF point from the Stills menu is absent from the Movie version of this menu, which also includes the two new entries, Movie Servo AF Speed and Movie Servo Track Sensitivity (described in more detail below). (Movies are often filmed with a fixed horizontal orientation.)

- The Initial Servo AF Point for Face Detect entry is absent from the AF 4 Menu, which is identical to the Stills AF 5 Menu.

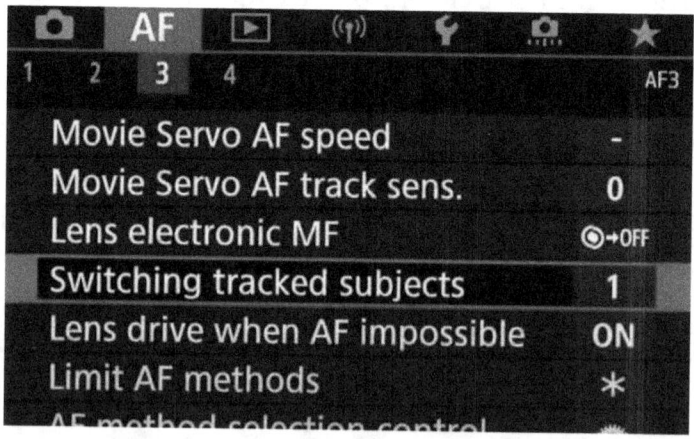

Movie Servo AF

When activated, this function uses just Movie Servo AF with either camera. Press the AF-ON button or push the shutter button halfway to start the autofocus. When in use, the focus is continuously adjusted without the need to push the shutter release partly. Tap the Servo AF icon in the lower-left corner of the LCD screen to lock focus or pause continuous focusing (for example, to stop the sound of the lens motor while it refocuses). Tap once more to resume. Additionally, if you press the MENU or Playback buttons or switch the AF method, Movie Servo AF will turn back on. With the help of the Movie AF Speed entry, which is discussed next, you may control how the camera reacts.

Movie Servo AF Speed

When Movie Servo AF is set to Enable, this option is available. The feature is also activated when utilizing USM or STM-powered lenses introduced after 2009. In addition, you have the following options:

- **When Active:** Always On automatically activates the AF adjustment speed setting before and while filming. The speed adjustment is only active when recording video when you select the During Shooting AF option.

- **AF Speed:** Click SET after selecting this choice. Then, using the touch screen, QCD-1, or directional controls, you can change the AF speed along a sliding scale from Slow (-7 to 0), Standard (0) to Fast (+1 to +2).

Movie Servo AF Tracking Sensitivity

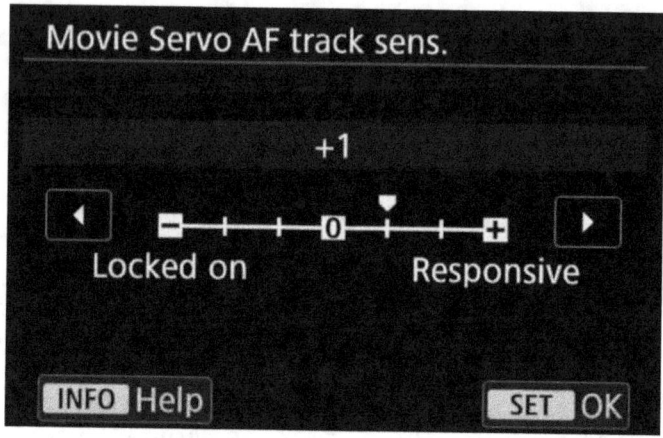

You can control how quickly the Movie Servo AF tracking system tracks a moving subject. First, the movie Servo AF needs to be turned on. The Tracking Sensitivity setting in the Autofocus 1 menu is comparable to this. Changing the tracking sensitivity can be helpful when a background subject enters the frame in front of the one you were trying to capture, just like with its still photo equivalent.

It helps pan as well. A sliding scale can be changed from Locked On (-3 to -1) to Responsive (+1 to +3) or standard at the 0 positions. Locked On instructs the camera to focus on the object in the frame, such as the football referee or a bystander in an urban setting. If a topic moves rapidly toward you or a new subject enters the frame, the camera's responsive settings instruct it to switch to tracking the object that is now in focus.

www.ingramcontent.com/pod-product-compliance
Lightning Source LLC
Chambersburg PA
CBHW070259220526
45465CB00004B/1673